T0194375

Profundity
One

Profundity One

David C. Franklin, M.D.

authorHOUSE®

AuthorHouse™
1663 Liberty Drive
Bloomington, IN 47403
www.authorhouse.com
Phone: 1 (800) 839-8640

Published by AuthorHouse 06/02/2015

ISBN: 978-1-4969-7096-1 (sc)
ISBN: 978-1-4969-7095-4 (e)

Library of Congress Control Number: 2015902595

Print information available on the last page.

*Any people depicted in stock imagery provided by Thinkstock are models,
and such images are being used for illustrative purposes only.
Certain stock imagery © Thinkstock.*

This book is printed on acid-free paper.

Contents

Dedication

THIS BOOK IS DEDICATED TO JIMMY AND JULIA
M. FRANKLIN, MY DECEASED PARENTS,

WHO WITH MODEST MEANS,

CARED FOR, LOVED AND INSPIRED
ALL NINE OF THEIR CHILDREN.

Introduction

Being black and striving to be a good physician in America during the early 80's presented some rather unique challenges not immediately obvious to all outside of the realm of medicine. This is all the more true for those who chose to embark on a career in surgery. The critical mind might counter with the observance that I was enrolled in only the third class to accept Afro-American students at the University of Alabama School of Medicine in Birmingham, December 1, 1971. This along with the fact that I hailed from an historically black university (Alabama State University), perhaps they could argue, flavors my perception of former events, which at best are isolated and in no way reflective of the national experience. Indeed, there may be some validity to these assertions. My intent, nevertheless is to present as factually as possible, personal experiences and observations from medical school, surgical residency and private practice. The reader is free to make his or her own conclusions as to merit and meaning of these recordings.

In many ways attending medical school at UAB was a unique experience for me. First of all it was the greatest academic challenge I had experienced to date. UAB was also my initial inter-racial educational environment. Though unique, I can't say that anything I experienced was surprising. To receive this one needs only focus on the era in which I was raised in Montgomery, Alabama. Called the "civil rights era", it allowed me the opportunity to witness in many ways the "freedom riders", "sit-in" demonstrations, "marches for freedom", and overt racism at it's worst. I was even privileged to hear in person the magnificent oratory of Dr. Martin Luther King, Jr. as he spoke from the capitol steps, about six blocks from my home. Unfortunately, I also felt the pain inflicted by the assassinations of President John F. Kennedy, Dr. King, Medgar Evers, and Robert Kennedy.

Consequently, I was not awed by the fact that only five of one hundred twenty three white students in my class would return my greeting, whether it was "What's happening", or "Good morning". Neither was I shocked when four of the six african American(AA) students in my class signed up to work with four separate groups of white students, only to return the following day to find all names stricken from the lists except their own. It did bother me, however, that we lost two AA students, not because they couldn't do the work, rather they succombed to the stress of a negative social climate. Though perhaps a friendship or two were fostered across the racial divide, towards the conclusion of our three year compulsory program, the common thread on both sides appeared to be respect.

Upon graduation I decided to pursue a career in general surgery and began scheduling interviews for residency positions. Ultimately I visited programs in Atlanta, Los Angelos, San francisco, Seattle, Portland, and Washington D.C. My interview at Georgetown university went unusually well and I guess I fell in love with "D.C.". In June, 1974 my wife Annie and I moved into an apartment in Fairfax, Va., about an hour's drive from "D.C." and adjacent to Fairfax Hospital one of my rotation sites. July finds me in the emergency room at Georgetown for an interesting six weeks rotation. Though I saw some surgical cases there the vast majority of cases were medical or gynecologic. One case I recall involved a twenty year old woman who presented to the ER accompanied by her male companion. She complained of several days of vaginal pain. She admitted to being sexually active and the rest of her history was basically normal with the exception of the pain and a thin straw colored discharge. Accompanied by the ER nurse I performed a physical exam which revealed moderate pelvic tenderness. After the patient was informed of the need for a pelvic examination, she concurred. As she was being prepared, I stepped outside of the draw curtains to inform her concerned boyfriend of our intentions. I returned and began the exam, completing the manual and then gingerly inserted the vaginal speculum. With the light of a goose neck lamp, I glimpsed something green in the vault of the vagina and immediately thought it to be pus and called for cultures. As I swabbed the area to obtain a specimen it became obvious that the green area was solid in nature. With a vaginal forcep and a better directed light, and some difficulty I was able to grasp a portion of the specimen as it rolled elusively about the vagina. As I pulled the specimen out the nurse was overcome with laughter(which she did her best to conceal) for within the forceps was an intact green grape. Further inspection revealed two more grapes which were similarly retrieved. The patient was given an injection and prescription for broad spectrum antibiotics and discharged quite gratified.

The highlight of my first two weeks at Georgetown was meeting Willie Blair, second year surgical resident from Mississippi. He was a stout, dark complected and bearded, jovial fellow who felt it his responsiblity to school me on the ends and outs of Georgetown. Willie invited Annie and I to his home in Alexandria, Va, where we met his wife Betsy and their two young children. The women and children took to the kitchen as we took to the den where Willie laid down Georgetown 101. He told me what attendings and residents to look out for, who had bitter dispositions, how to please certain surgeons, tricks of the trade and short cuts to various procedures. We hit it off very well and immediately were very comfortable and candid with each other. "I just say. yes sir, no sir, yes ma'am, no ma'am, and keep on moving. Tell 'm what they want to hear", Willie laughed. His remarks struck a chord within me and I felt compelled to respond. "I can't play it like that, Willie", I said. "I'll be the first to arrive in the mornings and the last to leave in the evenings, I'll work harder than anyone but that's all you get. No one can have my soul." "Well, more power to you if you're strong enough to play it that way, but that 's a hard row to hoe ", retorted Willie. "You see, I'm afraid to play these games, Willie, for I might forget where the game ends and true life resumes. If I am rejected for being me, then at least, I feel, I know the reason. But if I play the game, and play it well, and still I'm rejected; I just might have second thoughts." At the time I had no idea how prophetic these words would become.

After the E.R. rotation I moved on to Dr. John Coffee's service. An elderly gentleman, Dr. Coffee was an excellent surgeon, and a good teacher. He specialized in thyroid and parathyroid surgery and on most of his cases I first assisted. Dr. Coffee was distinguished for having the second largest parathyroid surgical series in the world. I enjoyed working with him and I learned a lot. He was indeed a scholar and a gentleman. We did so many parathyroid explorations that I began to think hyperparathyroidism was a common condition.

After two months It was time for my cardiovascular rotation with the chairman of the surgery department at Georgetown, Dr. Charles Huffnagel. I had been well informed that on this service I would not go to the operating room, instead would admit all patients, complete detailed history and physical exams, draw blood for labs, start IV's, do bleeding times, and any ancillaries required to prepare the patient for surgery. When the patient returned to the floor I would resume their care, and assimilate daily lab values, have all x-rays available and present all patients on evening rounds. There were 40-50 patients on the service at all times. Also, before I left this service, I was told, I would break down and cry in frustration from the sheer enormity of the work load. I psyched myself up to meet the challenge, determined to be the best first year resident ever to grace the service.

Very organized, leaving at 4 am I would arrive at Gergetown at 5 am, make rounds on all the patients, checking labs and collecting any recent x-rays and addressing any new problems discovered. This would continue until 12 noon, when I'd take 15 min to consume a sandwich and soda, finish rounds and wait for the new patients to arrive. Usually there were 5-8 new admissions, which kept me busy until Dr. Hufnagel and his enterage of three other attendees(partners), three upper year residents, and four medical students arrived. Rounds would take about 2 1/2-3 hrs, after which all admission duties would be completed. Reaching my apartment 11-12 pm, if hungry I would eat, then shower and go to bed.

My efficiency and stamina improved as the days ensued. Most of my patients were very gracious and many expressed appreciation and security in my self confidence. Some of the nurses, however did not share my patients sentiments. They were accustomed to telling the green 1st years what to do. I on the other hand had worked as a medical intern for six months in Montgomery, Al before coming to "D.C.". Having been on the front line I had seen many very ill patients recover, and unfortunately had seen some die. I was no longer green, and was not about to let someone tell me to do something I felt not to be in the patients best interest. The fact that I was black, I felt, in some instances exascerbated the situation.

One night on what had been a very busy day of ten admissions, one of whom I had yet to complete, we finished rounds ~11 pm. Dr. Hufnagel had asked me to write an order for 7 1/2 gr of caffeine for a patient who was lethargic from her analgesic (narcotic). After rounds I busied myself to admit my last patient, when I was approached by a nurse reportedly concerned about the caffeine order and its possible untoward effects on the patient's blood pressure. I explained to this nurse who also was a 1st year medical student, that caffeine is a xanthine derivative with mostly vasodilatory effects and at high doses could have mild vasoconstrictive properties. I reminded her that this order was from Dr. Hufnagel who undoubtedly had vast experience in using caffeine in these situations. She stated that she was not going to give the medication. I suggested that she take it up with Dr. Hufnagel for I still had an admission to complete. "But you're more available to me than he is", she retorted. "And I've answered your question to the best of my ability. Excuse me". I proceeded to admit my patient and got home about 1 am.

The following day after going through my morning routine, I glanced at my admission list and saw that a patient with the "subclavian steal syndrome" was to be admitted. Quickly, I went to the intern's room, reached for my Schwartz surgical text and began reading about the "sss" while eating my lunch. I heard someone open the door and looking up from my seat I saw a young white woman about my age, wearing a dress covered by an open white lab coat, sashaying deliberately towards me. "Hello, how are you"?, I said. Without responding she began to speak in a sing-song fashion reminiscent of her walk. "Dr. Franklin, I understand that you had a problem with one of my nurses last night". Having completely forgotten the incident concerning caffeine, she readily brought it to my recall. "Oh that was nothing", I explained and proceeded to rehearse the entire incident just as it had occurred. Expecting her to respond with something like "Well, don't worry I'll take care of it ". Instead, she said, "Well, if I ever hear that you talked to one of my nurses like that again..."

"What, I questioned, what are you going to do? "Oh, Charlie will hear about it", she mocked. "Let's not wait til next time, let us go now", I said, taking her hand and starting for the door. She snatched her hand free, blushed in the extreme and ran out the door. As she left I could not but notice we had attracted quite a crowd in the halls. I finished my lunch and reading on the "sss" and prepared for my new admissions to arrive. On evening rounds I expected to hear something from Dr. Hufnagel concerning the altercation with the nurse, but He said not a word.

The days moved on and I became increasingly more facile at meeting the demands of this very busy service. The nurses contrarily, became progressively more agitated and uncooperative, holding meetings, I was told, to decide what to do about me. They had no problem with the quality of my work, but insisted I had a bad attitude. I tried to recall instances where I had been rude, disrespectful or even condescending to the nurses. The cardinal sin I had committed, it seemed, was refusing to allow the nurses to manage my patients. Retrospectively, I nevertheless must admit, that merely touching the nursing supervisors hand (or any part of her anatomy) in later years could easily have provoked a lawsuit for harassment or even assault.

It was obvious to me now that there was a conspiracy on the part of some of the nursing staff to discredit me. Undoubtedly, I surmised they had gone to the chief as the supervisor had threatened. I decided that I would go to Dr. Hufnagel and let him hear the other side of the album before he left for a two weeks conference in Switzerland. After being on call one Friday night, having worked thirty two hours straight, I waited for the chief to arrive, hoping to speak to him before he began evening rounds. When I approached Dr. Hufnagel he agreed to speak with me, but informed me that he had an emergency case to perform. He asked me to attend to the floor while he took the oncoming junior and senior residents to the operating room with him. It was after 12 midnight when they finished and I saw Dr. Hufnagel in the doctor's dressing room. "Tell me what's going on, Dr. Franklin, my phone's jumping off the hook. What are you doing to the nurses?", he inquired. He smiled broadly and spoke with little concern or sincerity. "Dr. Hufnagel, if I may speak frankly, I don't feel that I'm doing anything to the nurses. They just don't like the idea of taking orders from an intern, especially a black intern", I responded. "Why, you are not the first black intern we've had in this program, we've had several", he countered. All I know is I'm committed to giving your patients the best care I can. Though I'm cordial, respectful and open to suggestions from the nurses, I feel that I should make the final decisions concerning management of patients since I am ultimately responsible for their care on the floor.", I explained. "Well, I' m going to Switzerland on tomorrow, and while I'm gone let's have a "be good to the nurses week", okay ?", he closed with a broad generic smile. As he left, so did I, most unfulfilled.

Though the atmosphere on the floors seemed thick enough to cut, no untoward events occurred until Friday when Dr. Hufnagel returned. Earlier during the day, I had twice been summoned by the nurses to redress and apply new ace wraps to the leg of an elderly and senile white female post-op a femoral popliteal by-pass procedure. Despite my best efforts at redressing the wound she somehow was able to get the entire dressing off, and worst of all, pick at her wound. The third time I redressed the wound I applied heavy adhesive tape atop the ace wraps, concluding that it would be difficult for anyone to remove the dressing. As I went about my daily duties, a smile covered my face as I realized that this was my last day on Dr. Hufnagel's service.

The entourage arrived about an hour late, but once rounds began, they flowed smoothly; that is until we walked into the little old ladies room. There she was, operated leg in the air, ace wrap dangling, scratching at the proximal portion of her wound. Immediately, Dr. Hufnagel went into a tirade. "This is unexceptable! Don't you know how to properly apply an ace wrap?", he demanded. The chief then began an half hour diatribe on how to apply an ace wrap, the risk of infection when the wound is violated, and excellence in general. Everyone on rounds seemed befuddled, wondering where he was going with all of this, especially since rounds were only half finished.

It finally dawned on me that Dr. Hufnagel, rather than teaching, was attempting to shame me and set me up for the breakdown. As he spoke he scrutinized me searching for any break in countenance. He too realized that this was my last day on his service, and was taking his best shot. The chief cared little about the quality of my work, or what I was learning, only how much butt I was willing to kiss to remain in the program. Mercifully, he brought his presentation to a close with "It's my job to make sure you do things right, isn't it, Dr. Franklin? "By now, instead of shame, I feel deeply violated and reluctant to open my mouth; for I knew that what would come forth would be far more. than the obligatory," Yes sir, Dr. Hufnagel." "Isn't that right, Dr. Franklin?", with emphasis. All eyes are now focused on me promptingly, "Say it, say it !", their faces seemed to say. The chief continued, "I said isn' t that right, Dr. Franklin !" I dared not speak. We stared at each other eye to eye for what seemed like an eternity. With a scowl on his ever increasingly red face, Dr. Hufnagel dropped his head and finally I spoke, "Next patient." We finished rounds and nothing was said, no good-byes, no thank you's, or other comments. Yet, I knew my career at Georgetown was mortally wounded.

Admittedly, the above recorded events make for interesting and sometimes hilarious reading and rest assured the complete story will be told in my soon to be published autobiography, "Hot Water Walking". Nevertheless, what the following pages will attempt to convey are the principles of life extracted from the quarry of these varied and sometimes turbulent experiences. Fortunately, I came to realize it's not about me and them, but me and Him.

Communication

What occurs when two or more spiritually connect and enter into earnest dialogue is nothing short of a miracle. Whenever hidden agendas, ulterior motives and concerns for self are laid aside in pursuit of a higher truth, a magic ensues which defies human understanding. Suddenly, answers elusive, to problems felt insurmountable, miraculously, and gloriously manifest themselves to the enlightened amazement of the conferring hearts.

No superior intellect is required to realize that it is the intecedent power of the Holy Spirit, dispatched through the devine decree of The Creator that shines the light that dispells the darkness in all situations as these. For the Father has said, "wherever two or more are come together in my name, there also will I be". And through Him are provided all of the wisdom, understanding, and knowledge to solve all problems.

Oh, how magnanimous is the Lord for he fulfills all of our needs!!

In all of our discourse, may we acknowledge the presence of, and abide under the influence of, the supreme illustrator, mediator, judicator, and final denominator, the Holy Spirit.

Of Storms And Fear

Blinding lightening flashes and deafening thunderbolts in the storms of life tempt us to seek refuge in the prison of fear. We must refuse this invitation at all costs for fear siphons our love, our power and destroys our sense of reasoning.

Fear is the antithesis of faith, the key that unlocks the blessings God has in store for his people. Walking in fear instead of faith, causes some to lie, some to steal, and some even to kill, thus losing the blessings God has provided us.

When in a storm, remember, you are there for a reason and only for a season. Perhaps, just perhaps there is some indispensable knowledge, the truth of which can only be etched in the topography of your mind by the indelible ink of life's storms.

Seek this wisdom fervently, within the hurricane's very eye; for only after it is obtained will there be deliverance <u>in the face of</u> the storm, or freedom to walk out of it.

When besieged by the tornadoes of life, give not focus or credence to fear but to the valuable lessons always hidden within these turbulent experiences.

dcf

Imperfect Seed

I'm just an imperfect seed planted in God's service to the production of good fruit through the grace and mercy of a glorious father.

Thank you, Lord, for accepting me just as i am with all of my defects of character, weaknesses and human frailities.

Thank you, God, for constantly shaping, molding, and fashioning me into a more useable vessel.

I'm forever grateful, Father, that you would endure the offence of moral mildew, decay and corruption; brave the putrefaction of self-ish fleshly desires, to reach and bring me your sick child, through the supernatural power of the Holy Spirit, to the throne of grace.

O'bless Your Holy Name.

Point of reference

Point of reference is everything. Why do I insist on
making myself the central figure, the focal point, from
whose limited perspective all things are viewed with
bird's eyes and tunnel vision. How much better to see
life through the eyes of the Lord who's view is
panoramic and visual acuity 20/20. Let's relinquish our
vision to the Lord and ask him to remove the blind spots,
optical illusions and distorted views He is sure to find
in all of us. The Father will doubtlessly make the
appropriate refractionary adjustments. With our
informed consents, He'll go one step further and turn on
us the micro-soul-a-scope, performing a divine resection
on the moral decay and infiltrative character
defects of our souls.

Supreme Pilot

Good morming Father,

Once again through grace and immeasurable love You have allowed me to experience another day. As the supreme pilot in my life You navigated me safely home on yesterday, brought me to a quiet idle; and at the appropriate time, shut me down for the night. Thank You, Lord, for peace in the midst of the storm.

With a loving touch, You awakened me this morning, extending to me yet another opportunity to witness the wonders of Your miraculous powers. Fine tune me now, O'God, with the instrument of the Holy Spirit.

Sit, if You will, Lord, in the drivers seat of my life. Take me where You want me to go. Show me what You want me to see, and reveal to me through Your manifest presence what it is that You want me to do.

Be forever, Father, the supreme pilot in my life; for in You, and You alone, is there peace and order in the universe.

The Right Thing

The very instant you resolve in the depths of your soul and with every fiber of your being to do the will of the Father, simultaneously, from the gates of hell is dispensed a decree naming you to the hit list of the prince of evil. Suddenly, unholy alliances of your friends and your enemies and all departments of the wicked powers that be unite to destroy before it bears fruit the tiny seed of righteousness that you have planted.

Though smooth sailing give way to stormy seas, take heed and recall the Lord will not suffer you to bear more than you can endure. And soon you will be heard to say, "the storm is passing over, Halleleujah".

The Request

O'Lord, grant unto me the love of compassion,
mercy, forgiveness, and the heart of service.

Father, give me eyes to see through the
smoke screens and illusions of life,
a mind to discern and cut to the core
of all situations.

And yes, Lord, make my hands and feet
strong, stable, swift, and facile, above
the demands of all present and future challenges.

Finally, Father, fortify your son with the spirit
of love and humility, courage and persistence,
resilience and diligence, that I will complete
the works for which you called me

Stress Creed Of The Afflicter

Appalled, angry, and disgusted over the advancements made by African Americans in this country, the oppressor is in search of the perfect weapon. Preferably, this would kill the adversary, if not kill then maim, if not maim then perplex and confuse, so as to rend him totally ineffective and paralyzed with doubt and fear.

Of course this weapon once engaged must make no sound and leave no trail of evidence to be traced to its employer. It must have universal applicability, effective at home and in the workplace, in a crowd or in solitude, destroying not only the individual, but all that supports him- his family, his community, his relationships, his career, and finally his self esteem.

"Oh where, oh where can I find such a gem", cried the afflicter. "Alas, it was right before my eyes all along. Somewhere I heard or read that my victim has a peculiar affinity towards hypertension and it's associated diseases of stroke, heart attack, kidney failure, and peripheral vascular occlusive disease of the lower extremities. So hard has been his way, it seems; historically deprived of water, food and shelter that his genetic pool has been programmed to atone for these deficits by favoring the retention af salt and water in his body."

"Stress, I'm told, intensifies this reaction, acutely through the fight or flight elicitation of adrenaline, and chronically, through the constant strain of cortisol. It's believed that this stress adversely affects the immune and central nervous systems of a being, increasing its chances of developing cancer, arthritis, peptic ulcer disease of the stomach and mental illness."

"Oh, it's all so clear to me now. In stress, I have at my disposal the ultimate weapon, powerful enough to stop the aspiring black in his tracks, reverse his achievements, and if necessary, take his life. I'll simply pump up the volume and turn up the heat in his workplace, in his home, and in his community. I'll wreak havoc on his finances. With the help of my colleagues, I'll rain stress upon the black man until he assumes his rightful place-or dies."

"Why, I'll even use his own brothers and sisters to implement my dastardly scheme. Now let me sit back and watch this deadly weapon kill and destroy, without lifting a single finger or dirtying my hands."

REALLY?

Wisdom

Wisdom is knowledge appropriate to the situation. Conversely, knowledge inappropriate to the situation is not wisdom but foolishness.

Facts used out of context lead to the wrong conclusions. Scripture erroneously applied to inappropriate situations is not righteousness but ignorance or deceit.

To be effective, knowledge most be tempered with the warmth of love to produce wisdom.

Father, give me the wisdom, understanding and knowledge, the spiritual discernment to behold You as the center of my universe, my focal point and point of reference to consider all things. O' bless your holy name.

Value System

I am either liberated or enslaved by my value system. This being so I must esteem above all things the fruits of the spirit.

Love, joy, peace, gentleness, goodness, longsuffering, patience and faith, these priceless gems will set me free, free to be the man God intends me to be, free to be the spiritual leader of my family, free to fight evil where ever it is found, free to draw others to Christ, free to resist the temptations of this world, free to secure a place for me in my Father's kingdom.

All that the world has to offer is not to be compared to these treasures for my eyes have not seen nor can my heart fathom the awesome splendor of the blessings my God has in store for me.

The fruits of the spirit are to be valued more than any worldly possessions, for the latter are fleeting, subject to the laws of decay and dissolution; but that which is gained through Christ endures forever.

How much better are the fruits of the spirit than the riches of the world. Enslaved is the man who values riches, power and influence above love for God, family, and fellowman. To control such a man is an easy task. All needs be done is threaten to take from him that which he values above all things, his earthly possessions, and he will do whatever to whomever, whenever it is commanded of him.

Make me aware O'Lord that whatever I pursue in perfection thereof, spend all of my thoughts and resources towards the acquisition of, the one and the same is my God and the object of my worship.

David C. Franklin, M.D.

Father God, through your sufficient grace, fill me with spiritual discernment that I am forever free of the idolatrous lure of this world. May I understand that my most precious possession is my soul, and may I willingly submit it to your service and care is my prayer.

Vision

Poverty is a major problem in black communities. It breeds hunger, low self esteem, teen pregnancies, high school dropouts, drugs and alcohol abuse, aids and other diseases, violence and crime; and finally, dysfunctional families and divorce. Despite discussions about reparations, it is highly unlikely that this government will make the necessary investment to help change this situation any time soon. I believe, nevertheless, that the community has self contained within its boundaries the very means for its own deliverance. A core of many formally educated, well trained and gifted individuals, skilled and unskilled laborers, sporting an annual payroll of over $600 billion dollars supports this position. Yes, there is enough money, enough education and technical expertise, and even enough wisdom; but what is missing in our communities is a spirit of unity. My clarion call right now to black communities, large and small, is for unity. Lay aside your differences and come together in love for our people. Many have died that we might have this opportunity.

Let's not blow it.

With the guidance and direction of almighty God, and the support and cooperation of unselfish individuals, we will activate the blessings of unity as promised in psalms 133. Unity is the key that unlocks the blessings God has in store for his people. The wealth, so sorely needed in the black community, will not be inherited as a gift from rich Uncle Sam, nor can it be obtained through illegal means. It must be earned through the creation and suppport of viable businesses in our country. Join me in this life's work. Bless and be blessed. Do right-get right. The time is now-just do it. With the determination of one whose mind is made up, let's roll, now!.

Vintage Divine

May the distiller of knowledge, wisdom and understanding find me a suitable vat in which to pour and store His spirit. May this be the controlling influence in my life. May it bless and direct my paths and the lives of others. May it inspire my works, protect my family, strengthen my faith, and forever cause me to reach toward and achieve God's divine purpose for my life.

Might I of no spirit partake except it be distilled in the house of the Lord. Of this may I drink long and deep that I might perceive and pursue the higher way. All praises to the King_ blessed is the name of the Lord.

Movement

There is a movement afoot in this country to reverse the progress made by black Americans. This progress, for the most part, was made possible through the sacrifice of life, blood, sweat, and tears of brothers and sisters during slavery and the civil rights era.

The movement is a distillation of much study, collaborative effort, loss of sleep, deliberation, and meditation on socio-economic warfare by both white and black oppressors of America. So insidious and effective is this campaign that most people have lost hope and cast their lots with the wicked, delivering to them on a silver platter all independent minded brothers and sisters who refuse to sell their souls for material gratification.

How does one survive in this jungle of deceit, where paper tigers abound, and spiritual corruption, embezzlement, blackmail and imprisonment are the order of the day? We must recognize the true prize in life as our souls and not the material enticements of this world. Remember, ultimate success is arriving at our death beds with our souls in tact.

Let us come together, anchor ourselves and grow deep roots in the word of God, yielding not to the temptations of this world. In so doing we learn to unite and provide a shield to all who refuse to be controlled by the promise of the "American dream". To turn our backs on those brothers and sisters assaulted by the prevailing system of dis-enfranchisement is to roll back the clock and negate centuries of achievements by black Americans. Immediate material rewards do not begin to justify the crippling effects on present and later generations of our children who will find themselves physical, socio-politico-economic prisoners simply because we sold our souls to the highest bidder.

Invitation

There is no experience more powerful, exciting and rewarding than to find one's self in the awesome presence of the Holy Spirit. When so blessed all personal agendas should be laid aside as we cease our "busy-ness" and focus all of our faculties on the very holiness, splendor, and life transforming power in our midst. As children of the most high, we, above all others should realize that it truly doesn't get any better than this. There exists no greater opportunity for salvation, healing, comforting, divine inspiration and instruction, and spiritual revival than when the Holy Spirit graces us with its miraculous appearance.

At all times and in all things may we learn to invite, recognize the appearance of, abide under the influence of, and receive the blessings of, the spirit of God. It is the desire of our Heavenly Father that we would learn of Him and come into His presence with thanksgiving and praise. It pleases Him that we accept His invitation to join the body of Christ, apply our gifts and talents to the furtherance of His kingdom; that we might be blessed with love, peace, joy, and life everlasting.

May we fail not, at all times, to accept this most precious of all invitations, and may we know that the best possible scenario for our lives is the one planned by our Heavenly Father. O'bless His Holy name.

How Great Art Thou

FATHER, God Almighty, how great art Thou.

Through your divine orchestration the heavens are
syncopated in the skies and according to your
supreme architectural design, your wisdom
and your might, the very foundations of the
universe are established.

How blessed am I to be your child.
O'bless your holy name.

Faith

No man comes to God except he be drawn. The Father made the first. That move was unconditional love. We responded with our hearts. The heart's response to God is faith(Adrian Rogers). Our move in response to the Master can be a small step or a giant stride, according to our faith. Faith, the substance of things hoped for, the evidence of things unseen; is also{according to Rev. Rogers) the currency of exchange in God's economy. With it I can purchase my heart's desires, according to God's will.

Clues

God works in mysterious ways _ but He leaves clues. In order to receive these messages from the Lord we must keep our antennas up at all times. Through meditation, prayer and sincere study of the word, we learn to keep still and quiet through the storms of life _ better able to hear god's instructions.

By mastering this concept and facing every situation, no matter how trivial or important, with the realization that I am never alone, but blessed with the constant presence of a divine silent partner possessed of flawless judgment; I assume more confidence and experience more peace in my life. Freed from the impossible task of considering every conceivable angle, aspect and minutest of details; I'm more productive as my human limitations are more than compensated for by my Lord and Saviour Jesus Christ, who alone is errorless and worthy of the first and last words in my life.

Choir Rehearsal

The choir room was abuzz with gossip, small talk, bickering, and a generalized spirit of contentiousness, when Sam, assistant choir director, after suffering all that he could endure, finally raised his voice in righteous indignation.

"People", he exclaimed, "let's not let him do this to us !! There's an evil spirit moving in this room tonight and we all know what satan is trying to do. He's moving amongst us trying to divert our attention from doing the work of the Father. Let us rebuke him in the name of Jesus. May we pray?"

"Father God, in the name of Jesus we ask that you dispatch the Holy Spirit to us now, castigate the devil and if you will, O 'Lord, drive him from our presence. Help us to realize that we are not here to pass the time or glorify ourselves but to magnify the name of Jesus. Consecrate us now O 'God that we may prayerfully accept this calling to work together in blessed peace and harmony and to love one another as sisters and brothers, lifting our unified voices in the most supreme of all human endeavors praising Your Holy Name." And the choir joined Sam in a chorus of amen. Amen.

Black People In Trouble

Black people in America are in trouble because, like the children of Israel, we've turned our backs on God who delivered us out of physical bondage. We've traded our spirituality for education, affluence and power. These we now worship and will do almost anything to acquire them.

WE ARE IN TROUBLE BECAUSE:
We are ignorant of our past and continually repeat the mistakes of our predecessors. There is no hunger or desire to know the truth about our ancestry, early civilizations and contributions to the world, the sacrifices of our foreparents, or their love for God and one another. Consequently, we are deceived by the literature of our oppressors and present day media, readily accepting the fallacies, omissions and negative stereotypes presented to us by historical books, newspapers, magazines, television and movies. Because we don't know our history, we don't know who we are, what we have done, are capable of doing, and finally, what we need to do to get where we want to go. And where is that?

WE ARE IN TROUBLE BECAUSE:
Our children are lost, over half raised by a single parent and some without either. Even when both parents are present, their ignorance of who they are and where they are going is more apt to be passed on to their off springs to further this cycle of doom. The message we send to our children is that love is not important. Just make it at all cost and the unpalatable fruit of this unrighteous philosophy has come home to roost in the form of black boys killing one another, black babies having babies, drug

infested black neighborhoods, alarming high school dropout numbers and unemployment figures for blacks- deplorable.

BLACK PEOPLE IN AMERICA ARE IN TROUBLE BECAUSE:

We don't love one another. Because we've bought into the negative stereotyping of our people, and because we are willing to make it at all costs, we find the easiest way to ascend the ladder of success is by stepping on the backs of our brothers and sisters. Our children see this and take note for they aspire to make it also. A form of hatred, a malignant jealousy has been spawned in the hearts of black Americans, and it might be said that these feelings we harbor for one another are the principle barriers to our success in this country.

WE ARE IN TROUBLE BECAUSE:

Viable black male/female relationships are at an all time low. The pool of elgible black males is reduced by imprisonment, homosexuality, interracial marriages and affairs, unemployment and lack of marketable skills, homicide, aids, other diseases and premature deaths. This disparity of too few black males to accommodate black females places an enormous burden on the survival of black courtships and marriages. As we assume the ways of the dominant society and resolve to make it at all costs our personal relationships become just another battlefield where our partners are enemies to be conquered, used, and when their purpose is served, discarded. Because of this warfare between the black man and woman, black families are suffering and divorces are rising. A cycle of broken families is sustained by children produced in these relationships. When will the black man and the black woman of America sit down as equals, abandon hidden agendas, check the egos in at the door; and enter into earnest dialog, heal old wounds and resolve to save our race by securing the black family structure?

BLACK PEOPLE ARE IN TROUBLE:

Because of a generalized lack of unity. We've decided it more profitable to align ourselves with the dominant society, giving full allegiance to the same, turning our backs to our heritage, our communities, and our children. It's no longer what 's best for my people but what's best for me. When given the

reigns of leadership and the responsibility of representing
our people we sell out at the first available opportunity.

WE ARE IN TROUBLE BECAUSE:
We don't hold ourselves or those chosen to represent us accountable
for our actions, consequently, we all suffer. A price should be paid by
those amongst us who sacrifice loyalty and integrity for personal gain.
Such actions should not be rewarded with re-election or promotion.

WE ARE IN TROUBLE BECAUSE:
We have not dedicated ourselves to solving the problems that threaten
the survival of our people. We lack vision and tend to be reactionary
rather than proactive. Little real progress is made in this mode.

BLACK PEOPLE ARE IN TROUBLE BECAUSE:
We don't think for ourselves. Others define for us what is beautiful,
intelligent, good, acceptable, and of course the antithesis of these,
which in this culture, we find most often attributed to us.

WE ARE IN TROUBLE BECAUSE:
We are enslaved by a defunct value system. Deciding too often to
serve the flesh instead of the spirit, we seem to have mortgaged all
that's dear, our relationship with god, our children 's future, our
heritage and legacy, all for the material enticements of this world.

BLACK AMERICANS ARE IN TROUBLE BECAUSE:
We've been deceived and hoodwinked to believe that what
the world offers is greater and more certain than what God
offers, namely eternal life and blessings so marvelous and
splendid our wildest imaginations could not fathom them.

WE ARE IN TROUBLE BECAUSE:
We have become complacent and trusting in the power merchants
of america, resting on the sacrifices and achievements of our
predecessors and as such are at risk of losing all we've gained.
Unfortunately, it may be necessary to lose all to gain true prosperity.

David C. Franklin, M.D.

WAKE UP, BLACK AMERICA!!

Accept this call to action. Raise high your antennas to the Almighty,
meditate and pray and listen for His divine instructions. Sit at the
conference table with your brothers and sisters and dialogue in
earnestness and truth. Come together in brotherly love and commit
to building strong black families and communities that will nurture
our children. Unity is the key as the psalmist exclaims in psalms
133: how good and pleasant it is for brethren to dwell in unity...
for there God commanded the blessings even life forever more.

The very instant we come together God will bless us with
His presence and usher in all of the necessary wisdom,
knowledge and understanding, inspiration and courage to
do the work of reviving our people. Let's get on it!!

Beyond The Fringe

Allowing God to order my steps on a daily
basis has rewards, perks, and benefits beyond the
fringe. He gives me courage and dispells
all fear. I can't worry and have faith too,
but must decide which will I do. Yes, He gives me benefits like
freedom, unlike that of the world, which is "free and dumb"
but free indeed; benefits like contentment- sufficiency
and peace in all situations. He gives me creativity,
strength, stamina, and spiritual
discernment. The Father enlarges my territory.
O'bless His Holy Name.

Aware

O'Lord, our God, how grateful we are for the opportunity to stand before Your presence this day. We are aware, Father, that only through Your endless love, Your boundless grace, and Your matchless mercy, are we blessed with the strength of body and the presence of mind to arise and meet You at this appointed time and place. O'bless your holy name.

We come finally, but so acutely aware that it was You who gave us life, and claimed us as Your own even before the union of our parents. It was You who taught us the meaning of love in that You first loved us, sending Your son to an horrific death on the cross that we might have life and it more abundantly.

We are aware, Father that it is Your supreme desire to quicken the seeds of perfection You planted within us, that in Your service we might have an abundant harvest and experience that joy and freedom that comes only through the full expression of one's God given talents. Thank You, Lord.

We come now, O'God, aware that the allure of sin and disobedience strives to separate us from You that we might fail, that we might hate, that we might covet, that we might lie, that we might die.

Ultimately, we are aware, Master, that we struggle not with flesh and blood, but principalities and evil in high places. In and of our selves, we have not the power to resist these forces. Victory in this war demands total immersion in Your word, continual prayer, abidance in the Holy Spirit, and sincere fellowship with true believers.

Strengthen us now, O'Lord; draw us ever closer to You. Help us develop discipline and passion, diligence and power in our spiritual lives. For we are aware, Father, in this only is victory. O'Bless Your Holy Name.

Encounter

100 men in prayer was founded in Plymouth, North Carolina, October 5, 1998. Having been involved in men's ministry for about six years in Birmingham, Alabama prior to moving to Plymouth; I had spoken to several men about the desirability of starting such a group. After two years, four men finally met at the fourth street school and something miraculous happened. The holy spirit filled the quite spacious room in which we met. Brothers began to testify of the goodness of the lord; and how he had delivered us from sin, within and without and from dangers, seen and unseen. We pledged allegiance and devotion to the spirit of unity as expressed in psalms 133. We discussed and adopted the principles of brotherhood and promised to be brothers, one to another, in the name of Jesus. In leaving, we prayed and agreed to bring someone new to the meeting each Monday night. Our ranks quickly swelled to a roster of 192 brothers with as many as seventy-five men attending most nights.

We acknowledged that we lived in a poverty stricken region of the state and many critical needs of the people were not being met by the county or state. We resolved to address these needs through providing monetary and general support to the youth, the poor and disadvantaged, the elderly, and the previously incarcerated. It soon became blatantly clear that we did not have the resources to fund these programs out of pocket though we did the best we could. The problem was poverty and the only solution was the creation of wealth through the establishment of viable businesses in our communities. We set about research to determine what businesses might be successful in this area.

One brother in particular, a retired New York police officer, and plymouth native felt that a high quality, destination restaurant would be well received by the residents of the immediate and adjoining areas of the state. Having run a successful restaurant and catering business in new york, an excellent chef indeed, the brother agreed to operate the restaurant for 100 MIP. He felt that the all but abandoned downtown plymouth located on the roanoke river could provide a unique ambiance for the restaurant and great investment potential for future appreciation. Building a second floor to the proposed site and the use of clear glass on the water side would provide a breathtaking view of the roanoke river as one dined in true elegance. More than once the brother called (six am on one occasion) to impress upon me the feasibility and indeed urgency of acquiring this property. "after all," he said, "they're not making any more riverfront property." I asked the brother to enter into negotiation with the owner of the site.

During this period I was employed as staff surgeon of Washington County Hospital in Plymouth. A part time position was also filled as physician for the Tyrell county corrections facility. Once a week I would drive the forty miles to Colombia, North Carolina, site of the prison, and see inmates practically all day. One day I will never forget I finished early and started my drive back to Plymouth. Leaving Columbia the next town one encounters is Creswell, then Roper and finally Plymouth. As I was leaving Creswell, there appeared on highway 64 an elderly white man "thumbing" a ride. He was leaning back with his thumb up-raised as I approached. I smiled at the savvy of this old man out there flagging a ride on that dangerous stretch of highway. I drove on by for I had never picked up a hitchhiker in my life. Suddenly something seemed to say. "pick up that old man". I found myself pulling over to the side of the road. Looking through the rear view mirror I could see the old man walking hurriedly towards my car with quite a noticeable limp. I backed up, stopped and the old man got in. I said, how you doing, sir? I'm David Franklin. "I'm going to Roper", he said. "Going right through there", I remarked. The old man began to talk. "Now over there", pointing to the right," used to be the biggest plantation around here. The town of Roper sits on what used to be the Cabin Creek Plantation. I know because my uncle used to own it. My name is Blount. Where you from?" Queried the old man. "I'm in Plymouth",

I replied-"been there for about three years". "Plymouth", remarked the old man, "that's a pretty little town but the people have no appreciation for it". "That's true", I agreed. "I remember I used to eat at a restaurant there", the old man went on. "It was right on the river. The food wasn't about anything but the scenery was good. But they didn't do it right. Shoulda had glass on the back so you could look out on the river and watch the snakes swimming". By this time we pull up to roper and the old man says, "I'm going to the post office." I turned left along side the post office, stopped and bidded the elderly gentleman farewell. "Have a good day, Mr. Blount, I enjoyed talking with you." "Yeah, you too", he said getting out of the car. With the door still open, the old man bends forward, looks me square in the eyes and exclaims., "By the way, let me know when you open up that restaurant".

Betrayed

Betrayed – Oh what a feeling

Betrayed – Sometimes it leaves you reeling

Betrayed – Appearing to give though stealing

Betrayed – Feigning love when hate concealing

Betrayed- To kill and maim they came

Betrayed – Friend and foe the same

Betrayed – At my feet the blame

Betrayed – Fanning hate's old flame

Betrayed – O' how can this be

Betrayed – Seduced of loyalty

Betrayed – How? I could not see

Betrayed – In the name of charity

Betrayed – To eat from this plate

Betrayed – Served of friend and mate

Betrayed – Tempts it though to hate

Betrayed – Seal it not my fate

Deceptions

We are deceived whenever our perceptions in consideration of any question, are esteemed above our spiritual discernment, for the reaper knows well how to appease our senses. Many are the false roads which lead us away from the Lord and thus a more perfect expression of ourselves.

We are deceived when we hold on for dear life to that which we possess in fear of losing, for to freely give is to please the Father, the imminent source of all blessings.

Victims of deception are we when we resist positive change in support of the status quo, simply to maintain some perceived material advantage.

Deceived we are when lead to believe the grass is greener, and food from the table more delectable in the camp of the oppressor. As such, we abandon the causes of our people and adopt the policies and agendas of the despoiler, desiring that he from his plate might dispense unto us a crumb or two. And when our usefulness is outlived, deceived are we to perceive safety and favor in the house of our co-conspirators.

Deception revels in our destruction as true love, dampened by years of routine and familiarity is traded for the temporary lift and euphoria of a red hot affair. Steep and long is the fall of one who succumbs to this subterfuge.

That there is no hereafter, no life after death and no final judgment_ that to live well is to experience as much pleasure and acquire as much material wealth as time on earth will allow; is the greatest deception of all for it robs us of our most precious gift, eternal life with the Father.

God's Man

To some he may appear a bit strange, peculiar and perhaps odd. Yes, (o-d-d-d). The "o" is for obedience to follow God's commands. The first "d" is for discipline to study God's word continually. The second "d" is for diligence to stand on God's word in all situations. The final "d" is for deliverance from all dangers, seen and unseen.

God's man knows that no weapon formed against him shall prosper. The Lord goes before him, enlarges his territory and fights all of his battles. He is possessed of the most powerful force in the universe-the word of God. God's Man.

He knows how to laugh.
He knows how to cry.
He knows how to live.
He knows how to die.

He knows how to love
and love how to receive.
He knows you succeed
only when you believe.

He knows when to take on
and when to put away.
He knows when to leave and
He knows when to stay.

His heart is clean
and his spirit renewed.

For the right cause
he is always moved.

Blessed are they
who call him friend,
for he will be with them
until the very end.

He loves his wife
and his family.
He strives with his brothers
for God's unity.

He's always on time
and in due season.
For the things he does
he has good reason.

For reality he lives
and not the perception.
He has no need
for lies and deception.

In all he does
he seeks God's favor.
For the Master's word
he truly doth savor.

He values salvation
above all things,
and never seeks to live
above his means.

He knows it is better
to give than receive,
To fill the need
and pain to relieve.

David C. Franklin, M.D.

God's man is the full measure of a man.
God's pleasure in a man.
God's treasure in a man.
God's man.

Heed

In life there will be trials and tribulations, and oft times sufferings. When one in the midst of a storm is approached by one who knows little of the bludgeonings of life, in a vain attempt by the latter to administer to the former; what occurs is catamount to pouring salt in the wound.

When one who fought the good fight, stood against all odds, survived and sometimes thrived, hears the quaisi-intellectual pontifications of so called leaders who spend their entire lives articulating "THE PROBLEM "; what occurs is equivalent to forcing one to watch "ROOTS" year after year after year.

Challenge

I <u>must</u> not allow the threat of nor

the potential for disaster to rob me

of the certainty and reality of joy.

I <u>will</u> not allow the narcotics of

mediocrity, complacency and

compromise to anesthetize, paralyze

And numb the life out of me.

Inner Portrait

Come forth, come forth, work, work within me.

Validate my existence on these pages of history.

By whatever means, express real essence,

the twain, my dullness and rare luminescence.

Craft of mine in all you do

ABOVE ALL THINGS PRESENT ME TRUE.

Jealousy

When jealousy is found infesting and possessing the heart
of one drawn near, though painful, nevertheless, it is
necessary to extend distance to him once held dear.

For the fires of no other hell burn as intensely and consume so
completely as jealousy. Subjugation, domination, devastation and
disaccreditation are the obsessions and passions of jealousy.

Devoid of conscience and moral restraints and uninfluenced by
the dictates of honor and fair play, jealousy seeks satisfaction by
any and all means necessary. Whether cleverly disguised in a cloak
of self righteousness, or flashing in its cute birthday suit, jealousy
is a child of Satan and claims dominion as its singular purview.

Live!!

Stop existing in fear and the probability of defeat.

Start living in faith and the absolute certainty of victory!

Birmingham Flight

On a mid-August Sunday morning of 1998 in the small town of Plymouth, North Carolina, my wife Annie and I along with our twelve year old son David, jr, arose in our home, an ancient(1867) well preserved two storied structure, less than one block from the small dowmtown district which ran parallel to the Roanoke river. Having lived here for over two years, we ordinarily would have been preparing for church on this Sunday morning. As it was, however, a recurring feeling of dread struck my core, as I realized that on tomorrow in Birmingham, Alabama, I would be appearing as the defendant in my first malpractice law suit.

After a quick breakfast, including coffee for me, we loaded our luggage into my '94 Suburban diesel and set off for Raleigh, North Carolina, the closest regional airport. As I drove this distance of about 160 miles of mostly interstate, my mind, as if to avoid the unpleasantness of the present and the potentially more painful and uncertain future, took the path of least resistance and went into a fast reverse. It stopped in the year 1967 in my hometown of Montgomery, Alabama at Booker T. Washington High School. It was my senior year when I received a full four year scholarship all expenses paid offer from Cornell University. Refusing the offer, I instead attended the local historically black Alabama State University on scholarship. "Wonder what would have happened, I mused, had I gone to Cornell?"

The clock in my head sped ahead to my senior year at (Bama State) when my fraternity adviser nominated me for a Ford Foundation Minority Student Grant. After flying to New York City, having my interview and meeting some very inspiring and interesting students, I returned to

Montgomery. About two months later I learned that I was a recipient of one of the Ford grants and could attend the university of my choice, all expenses paid including a generous living stipend. The only stipulation was that I pursue the doctorial degree and teach on the collegiate level. Choosing Michigan State University to seek a PhD in biochemistry, all that remained, it seemed, was to finish my undergraduate courses, have a good summer and begin graduate studies in September, 1971.

Driving on, now about 130 miles from Raleigh, my mind reflected on an incident which changed the course of my career. It was early March, 1971, when I spied in the distance walking towards me on the Bama State campus, a good friend and fellow chemistry major, Anthony Jones. As we approached one another I asked him where he was headed. Anthony stated that he was going to a seminar on medical school and suggested I accompany him if I wasn't busy. With no classes scheduled for the next two hours I walked with him to one of the lecture halls in the basic science building. Down front were two white haired caucasions, whom we later learned to be Dr. Margaret Clapper, dean of the UAB School of Nursing and Dr. Henry Hoffman, chairman of the the department of anatomy, UAB School of Medicine. Anthony and I listened attentively as they conveyed the statistical need for more black physicians in the United States(esp. Alabama), the prerequisit courses and time frame for application, and finally what one could expect once he or she is accepted to the UAB School of Medicine. Having clearly heard them state that one should apply to medical school at least two years prior to graduation, we nevertheless approached them after their presentation, inquiring as to the possibility that we might be accepted in the UAB Fall Class 1971, knowing we'd be leaving Bama State in 2 1/2 months. "Well, ordinarily your chances would not be very good", replied Dr. Hoffman, "but this year we are constructing a new basic science building scheduled for completion by November. Consequently a second class will start in December. Why don't you guys come up for interviews?"

Just like that, two weeks later Anthony and I found ourselves in my old Pontiac Catalina headed for B'ham and scheduled interviews for entrance into medical school. After six separate meetings, numerous questions and reviews of our transcripts, at the end of the day we were informed that I was acccepted but Anthony was not. Being quite fond of Anthony I truly regretted the latter, but soon found myself grappling with the issue of whether to relinquish my Ford Foundation Grant at Michigan State to attend the UAB School of Medicine, where at that point the only assurance of financial aid was a general statement made by many that the university had never lost any student because of financial difficulties. After much deliberation, several weeks later I decided that I would prefer taking care of patients over teaching biochemistry at the collegiate level.

As I motored on towards Raleigh, my thoughts sped on down memory lane where upon graduation from Bama State, a Macy's Grant of $1000 afforded me the opportunity to take undergraduate courses in human physiology and human gross anatomy at UAB. Living with my uncle Channel Floyd and his wife Louise(an excellent cook) I had no financial obligations. However, when the summer of '71 ended I took a job as research assistant to a microbiologist at UAB and moved into an apartrment. I called my fiancé, Annie, whom I'd been dating for about 15 months. I told her how much I loved and missed her and she confirmed the same for me. I drove to Jackson, Alabama(~250 mi), picked Annie up and brought her back to B'ham where we were later married.

December quickly rolled around and soon I was knee deep in medical school. What impressed me most was the sheer volume of four years of work our professors squeezed into the three year compulsory program. Only the third class at UAB to admit black students there being six in our class of 129, I found most of my white counterparts cold, aloof and basically unfriendly. Only five of 123 would return my greeting whether "What's happening?" or "Hello, how are you?". When an African American student signed his or her name to a list of white students in order to share a cadaver in gross anatomy, the next day found all names stricken from the list except their own. Two of my fellow black classmates were lost to attrition primarily because they could not function well in such a strained environment. Though not the most pleasant of experiences, time passed, and soon I was graduating somewhere in the middle third of my class. After deciding on a career in general surgery, I began to line up interviews at prospective programs.

My first stop was nearby Grady Hospital, Emory University, Atlanta, Ga., where the director all but guaranteed me a first year resident position. It was then on to California(Annie and I drove the distance in 2 days) where I interviewed at both UCLA and USC as well as Martin Luther King, JR. hospital. Driving up the coast we assessed surgical programs at the University of Sanfrancisco Moffit, as well as university programs in Seattle, Washington and Portland, Oregon. Though on a very limited budget, we drove all the way back to L.A., where we stayed for one week, resting and taking in some of the city.

Upon return to Alabama, one week later found me and my brother James, in Washington, D.C., where I interviewed at Georgetown University. The program looked good and I think I fell in love with "D.C." I entered the surgical residency at Geogetown where I remained for two years, completing my final three years at York Hospital, York,Pa.

Throughout my training and career as a black student, resident, and surgeon I experienced many things which had more to do with who instead of what I was.

Arriving at the airport in Raleigh my mind flipped back to reality. I was angry, and frustrated and a bit fearful as I reflected on the horrors of the malpractice courtroom I had heard about over the years. I was convinced and knew I was not guilty of any crime in my discharge of medical care to the plaintiff, instead was the victim of a malicious plot by the black referring physician, the racist surgeon who subsequently reoperated on the patient and the hospital which had denied me hospital privileges for two and a half years though I was the youngest board certified general surgeon in Birmingham at the time. Only through the threat of a law suit was I given admitting privileges at this hospital situated in the heart of the black neighborhood.

As the plane ascended to 30,000-35,000 feet I felt a trans formation occurring inside of me, as all fear, frustration, and anxiety was dispelled from my being, replaced by a consuming peace, courage and clarity. I was ready for battle. The man exiting the plane was not the one who boarded it in Raleigh.

Though two physicians participating in the care of the plaintiff testified against me, against all odds I won the case. All praises be to God. See details in forth coming autobiography, "Hot Water Walking".

Men's Ministry

Through God's intervention in the men's ministry I came to know just who I am.
There with my brothers the Holy Spirit revealed as quiet as kept we were all in a jam.

God brought us together, molded us and strengthened our bonds of love,
taught us how in the face of the storm to have the heart of a lion but the peace of a dove.

We learned to trust, commit and serve one another and true brothers how to be.
Through trials and tribulations we held true to our pledges of loyalty.

Because of the ministry we no doubt will never be the same. Being true brothers in God's service is our only claim to fame.

Notes

1. Dad's gift to me in his death-ushered in a strong desire to know and abide in the presence of the Lord.
2. Understand that the supreme event in life is to be in the presence of the Lord. I must stop whatever I'm doing and witness the awesome power, magnificent glory, boundless grace, matchless mercy, and endless love of Almighty God.
3. Record these experiences immediately for they are precious and fleeting. I must not trust my mind to record these jewels for once they are lost I may not be able to recover them.
4. My storm is my Jericho, the stronghold which binds and imprisons my spirit. The secret to overcoming the hurricanes of my life is to walk through the turbulence into the storms very eye, pick up the wisdom that quiets the wind and unlocks the next chapter in my life.

Of Gifts And Talents

All of us are unique – each endowed with our own special gifts or talents. There is at least one thing each of us can do better than anyone else on the face of this planet.

Unfortunately, these gifts are seldom recognized, lying dormant within their possessors for a life time. When hidden talents are revealed by the lord, procrastination and slothfulness work together to prevent their complete development and full expression. And still they lie dormant.

Rarely, when one recognizes, exercises and develops these special abilities, too often he or she lends them towards selfish motives and not to the furtherance of God's kingdom. This culminates in stunted growth, decreased effectiveness and ultimately, loss of the gift.

Ignorance of who we are as children of God make us easy prey for the evil forces of this world, which strive unceasingly to cause us to feel useless, worthless and helpless. Once we buy into this lie of Satan's it is almost impossible to recognize, develop fully, and use appropriately, the gifts our Father has so lovingly bestowed upon us.

Be not deceived, but ever aware that the Father took a hands on approach in our creation. Consequently, He is uniquely cognizant of what gifts and talents He placed in all of His children and how best to perfect that which He has crafted. It is the Master's desire that the seeds of perfection He planted within us should spring forth to a bountiful harvest, the fruit of which shall nourish His kingdom.

Concerning the issue of gifts and talents, let us seek wisdom through the study of God's "how to manual for our lives", the bible. It will teach us how to recognize, develop, maintain and perfect that which our Heavenly Father has placed within us. Then one day we will be blessed to hear "well done my good and faithful servant…".

Paper Tigers

Paper tigers leap from the jungle at any time to threaten my world.

Paper tigers roar and growl but unlike the saber tooths have no true power but that which I forfeit them in my spiritual weakness.

The purpose of paper tigers is to incite fear, confusion, panic and chaos.

The snarl of the paper tiger vies for my attention, that I might cease my efforts in doing the work of the Lord; that I might be arrested in spiritual growth and robbed of my souls salvation.

With the help of the Lord let us yield paper tigers null and void.

Power Of Faith

There are times in life when the cutting edge gets dull, when enthusiasm and zeal can not be found, and the very flame of our faith seems to flicker. Some call it chronic fatigue, others burn out, stressed out, washed out, and played out. Whatever the term applied to this condition, it is more than anything, a perceived loss of the power and ability to achieve our goals.

Let us not deny the existence of these feelings when besieged by them, for such is to invite more serious derangements as anxiety and depression. Understand, and we must, that our situation is not unique, nor are we the only ones subject to occasional weariness for even our Lord the perfect Christ, retreated from Galilee, the constant healing of the people and the relentless pursuit of the Pharisees and Sadducees into the coasts of Tire and Sidon (Matt 15:21-31). A reflection on the indifference of Jesus towards the poor Canaanite woman who broke his retreat by fervently beseeching Him to heal her demon possessed daughter, only reveals the human side of the Messiah for He was fatigued. Nevertheless, the woman showed great faith, and was not dissuaded by the irreverence she received. So strong was her faith that it cut like a knife through the apathy of the Christ, and He was moved to unleash healing power on the woman's daughter. It was faith (obviously) that gave this woman the power to pray unceasingly to the Master. It was faith that moved Him to heal her daughter. It was faith that dispelled the weariness and quickened the healing power within the Christ. So

revived was He according to Matthew He ascended into a
mountain in Galilee and healed all who came unto Him

Faith is the key to empowerment. When our tank runs
low, let us fill up with the word of God, for faith cometh
by hearing and hearing by the word of God.

Prepare A Place For Him

Before we make any decisions, resolve to engage any activity, choose a mate or a business partner, accept any official position, adopt any life style, sit at any conference table, enter into any dialogue or debate, celebrate any victory, or mourn any defeat; let us seek counsel with the Master for it is He abiding within us that is stronger than the world. It is He that has the power to bring all things into being and He that provides the spiritual discernment to make all things clear.

May we through prayer and meditation continually seek His divine presence and prepare a place for Him in every workshop and forum. Adorn the conference table with the centerpiece of righteousness and integrity, and let the atmosphere abound in truth, honesty, commitment and trust. Serve up adequate portions of love, faith, kindness and patience and the supreme pilot will surely take a seat, His presence revealed through the assumption of unity and cooperation, the issuance of progress and order, and the dissolution of doubt, fear and ignorance.

Remember, He will not grace a table defaced in selfish ulterior motives, hidden agendas, lies, and deceit; nor will He sit with persons whose eyes wink and whose hands curiously descend beneath the table in search of deals. Of these may we not engage, but at all times have the wisdom to prepare a place for Him who can do all things but fail. O 'bless His Holy Name.

Real Man

Not too ashamed to cry
Not too afraid to die

Not too puffed up with Pride
Neither deflated with hopelessness

Honest enough to say I don't know
Not only sires but trains his children
In the way they should go

Knows which battles to engage
Not defined by his possessions

Seeks favor with God rather
Than popularity with man

Power Of The Anointing

Never mistrust or doubt the

power of the anointing. God has

placed this power within the

inner person of all called unto

His purposes, for it is more than

sufficient to the completion of

All vision.

Ropadope

Now I know we been brainwashed, lulled to sleep with the lullaby,

Conned and scammed, hoodwinked and ripped with the rip van winkle of the mental ropadope.

But let it go, bro, for it's time to grow, and don't you know that when we grow, we raise the nation. Rise!!

Spending Time

May I spend less time asserting

who I am, and more time improving

the quality of my work, that I

might realize the goals of my

life.

Survival Anthem Of The Black Man

Black man in America, arise and assume your rightful
place. Sit at the head of the family table and accept
the responsibilities of leadership. Understand
that your task is an onerous one for your course
heretofore has not been charted. No leisure will be afforded you as you plan your strategy; and paranoid you are
not as you realize that the "powers that be see physical
psychological, social and economic destruction of the
black man, as the key to subjugation of the black race.

You must survive for there is much work to be done, and
the baton of completion has been passed to you by those
who gave life, blood, sweat and tears to keep you in the
race. Life is serious business, and there is no time for
casual meandering. To survive we must divest ourselves
of the "I-me-my mentality", and adopt a "we-us-our philosophy"
for a man who stands alone is an easy target. Moreover, universal law
dictates that where there is unity and one accord,
wisdom, knowledge, and solutions abound.

The survivor has his priorities in order, his value system reflecting
the importance of God, family, fellowman, career and self in
proper perspective. There is no slothfulness in the survivor. He
is willing to work, understanding that service is a prerequisite
of leadership. Realizing that leading, matriculating and growing
amidst a struggle for survival is an ordeal, the survivor learns
how to counteract the ill affects of the stresses in his life. He
meditates on the word of God, eats right, gets proper rest and re-

59

laxation and develops flexibility in approaching the challenges
In His life, never enslaving himself to any particular lifestyle.

The survivor has a hunger for truth, searches it out and makes it
an integral part of his life, no time for deceptions or illusions.
He fills his heart with love, both for god and his fellowman; and
never forgets in the heat of the struggle, why it is that he
must survive to do the will of the father.

So yes, black man, survive. But far more do, thrive;
and fulfill your destiny in the Lord.

Thank You

Father God, how wonderful it is to come into your presence
this morning. Though my faculties fail me and my humanness
hinders me in my efforts to fathom the unsearchable riches you
have bestowed upon me; suffer me, Lord, to say-thank you.

Thank You, Master for blessing me in my being, becoming
and going forth. Thank You, Abba, for glancing past
my wretchedness and focusing on my necessities.

Thank you! Thank You, Father, for claiming me as your child,
for life, health and strength and the provisions there of, for my
soul's salvation through Christ, for the holy word which guides
my steps, for forgiveness through grace and immeasurable love,

For the faith that sustains and empowers me, for family,
friends, brothers and sisters in christ, for the constant
presence and anointing power of the holy spirit,

For peace in the midst of the storms of life, for life's work,
recreation and relaxation, for the fruits of the spirit,

For your chastisement and correction, for loving me more
than I loved my self, for being my friend when I was your
enemy, for liberation from the miry dungeons of sin,

for a point of reference to consider all things, and most of all, Father,
I want to thank You for just being God. O' Bless Your Holy Name.

The Million Man March

The million man march was something to
behold, O'How I wish I'd been there,

To see black brothers noble and bold, their pledge for
atonement declare.

What pride order and unity they displayed in the face
of negative criticism,

Leaving the world awed and dismayed o'er their
spiritual collectivism.

Inspired of God there can be no doubt
the brothers were in one accord.

Forgiveness and healing was what it was about,
as they thanked and praised the lord.

In rare form was Farrakhan, courageous righteous
and true,

Expounding on what must be done and how to do
it too.

Hold on, brothers. Hold on brothers-to the spirit
of that day.

Follow through, brothers. Follow through,
brothers-on your pledge in every way.

The Picture I See

Why do I blame others for the way I view them,
when it is my own vain imaginations that
frames the picture I see.

May I learn to look and see, not glance and
glimpse into the very heart of an individual.

Teach me to see as you see, Father, for your view is
panoramic, seen through an all encompassing lens.

Remove the optical illusions, visual defects, and
faulty perceptions for which I am prone.

Father, teach me to laser in on and focus on the
good in all individuals I meet, that they might
perceive some merit in what I do and glorify your name.
Amen.

Rejoice

Lament not the lows of the now and then,

rather rejoice for the coming when.

The Joyful Life

I must not allow the threat and potential
for disaster rob me of the certainty and reality
of joy.

I will not allow the narcotics of mediocrity,
complacency, and compromise to
anesthetize and numb the life out of me.

Already There

In deference to my faith I live in the already as opposed to
the not yet and claim victory this day.

Through my darkness and my weakness, He shines forth
his marvelous light and manifests His awesome power.

He could speak it into existence, yet He prefers to
use imperfect beings to do perfect work. Thank
You, Father. O'Bless Your Holy Name.

Abba

This is the day that You have made, let us rejoice
in it and be exceedingly glad.

We invite, acknowledge, abide, and abound in
Your presence.

Thank You for Your divine dominion in our
lives, for Your love, concern, and caring.

Thank You for the proper means to an end
and a way out of no way.

Blessed be the name of Yaweh.

Happy Birthday, Annie, My Love!

God bless the day Mama Rena birthed you into this world. I thank my heavenly Father for molding and shaping you into one of the most beautiful and virtuous of all his creations. Blessed am I that you somehow found favor and shined your love on such a wretch as me.

Words have not the capacity to describe the depth of my love for you. Your outer beauty rivals all I've seen, second only to your beauty within.

Over the years you have been the quiet strength that has kept our family intact. You have loved me through good times and bad and tribulations many, though never wavering. My desire is to love you more, to treasure you and bestore upon you all befitting the queen that you are.

On this the, day of your birth, may The Lord bless you with an extra portion of His Grace that you may have continuous love, joy, peace, prosperity, and a long healthy life.

Please know here now and always that I love you, want you, need you and appreciate all you do for me and our family.

May the Father grant me the right heart, mind and strength; develop within me the discipline and diligence to love and treasure you all the more and be a blesssing to you Annie- my heart, my queen.

ALL MY LOVE

David

"Sail On, Brother Nelson, Sail ON"

You prepared your ship well, using only the sturdiest, tried and proven elements in your structural design. The Master has provided a strong updraft lifting you swiftly and ever so higher to your appointed destination in the heavenlies. By now your spirit has been received by the Father and you've heard the long awaited words, "Well done my good and faithful servant." The celebration is on and though we are not there with you, our souls rejoice. We rejoice in the memory of your warm and geniuine smile, the softness and sincerity of your voice, the total engagement of your gaze, and the depth of your God inspired wisdom. You, more than most, understood that it is better to give than to receive. The spirit of love, commitment, loyalty, trust, confidentiality and service was stamped in your heart and felt by all those blessed to have been in your presence.

We, "100 MEN IN PRAYER" thank you for the "ships" you built and left with us. The "friendships" and the "relationships"_may they sail on forever, we pray. Thank you for the "HOODS" you left us-the "neighborhood" which we must develop in your memory, and the "brotherhood" which your life has charged us to perfect.

Yes, sail on, Brother Nelson, sail on, on a cloud in the sky, to your home on high.

For as you lived and died, through God's awesome plan, we've seen in the flesh, the full measure af a man.

Farewell, dear Nelson, fare-the-well in your home on high. May we see you there someday in the coming by and by.

William Henry Norman (Happy Jack)

William Henry was a godly man, so gentle and full of joy.

A humble man, a child of God-yes, the real McCoy.

Above all things Bro. Henry truly loved the Lord,

And with the Holy Spirit he was in one accord.

that we will miss him, this we know is sure.

For seldom have we seen a heart so clean and pure.

So sail on my brother, to your home on high.

We all hope to see you in the coming by and by.

We thank you, Happy Jack. All of us, your family, your beloved children, your church, your friends, and your brothers of 100 Men In Prayer. We shall forever be indebted to you for the loving light you shined on all of us. For teaching us how to love the Lord, to worship and praise the Lord in honesty and in truth, to continually give thanks and testify of the goodness of the lord and never be ashamed to tell the world what God has done for us. We will always love you, Henry, and though saddened at your departure, our hearts rejoice knowing that you are coming home to be with the Father and our Lord and Savior Jesus Christ. We love you William Henry. Peace.

Holy Spirit

Holy spirit abide with me this day

Enter now please and in my heart stay

Move as you will and do have your way

Speak to my soul and lead me I pray

Upon your appearance is infinite bliss

Clamorings cease-there's no better than this

Receiving not the spirit is truly remiss

Without the soul enters a woeful abyss

But the Holy Spirit is here. Rejoice, rejoice!!

Of all companions this is my choice.

In every heart let the Holy Spirit abound

Throughout the world no greater friend can be found

Gary's Homegoing

Gary Clagon was a man that I loved. He was my friend, my patient, one of my church elders, my brother in 100 Men in Prayer, and most of all my brother in Christ. Now I don't know why God would allow him to be taken away from us at such a relatively young age, in the prime of his life. But one thing I do know and that is – at the time of his departure from this world, elder Gary Clagon had grown into the full measure of a godly man.

Gary Clagon was a quiet, soft spoken man by nature, but he was courageous and bold in matters concerning the lord. One thing I shall always miss seeing is Bro. Gary entralled in the Holy Spirit, praising the Lord with a dance. It was spontaneous, authentic, explosive and intensely powerful.

Bro. Gary was full of love, love for his darling wife Etta, for his precious children, and all of his family. He had great love for his church which he served faithfully.

Bro. Gary loved 100 Men in Prayer and invested his time, resources and energies toward the furtherance of its projects. The brothers in turn learned to love and respect Gary, and he shall be missed by all of them.

Yes, Elder Gary Clagon was all about love, not just for those whom he was familiar, but for all of mankind. His love was an unselfish, unconditional, uncompromising, agape type love. He conquered self and pruned his priority tree of life to reflect God at the top, his family next, the concerns of his fellowman to follow and his personal concerns were placed at the bottom. Brother Gary was one of the few people I've known who mastered what Dr. Martin Luther, Jr. called the length, breadth and height of life. He easily negotiated the length of life, representing his inward concern for personal fulfillment, and moved on in to the breadth of life, which was his outward concern for the welfare of others. After receiving advanced degrees on this level elder Clagon was allowed to pursue the height of life, which was his upward reach for God. And now, having mastered all three dimensions of life and placing them in proper prospective, Bro. Gary has graduated into eternal life with the Father.

Truly, we thank God for allowing us to see in the flesh one who walked with the Lord. He was a cornucopia, an orchard of the fruits of the spirit. His love, joy, peace, kindness, goodness, longsuffering, patience and faith has blessed all of us. Thank You, Father.

I could go on and on talking about this man of God. But suffice it to say that at the time of his departure, elder clagon was a full grown godly man.

"Fly On Brother Gary"

So fly on Bro. Gary to your home on high.
We all hope to see you in the coming by and by.

Fly on Bro. Gary. You've taught us many things.
How in life we sometimes must mount up on eagles wings.

Fly on, Bro. Gary. You've completed the winner's race.
Now it's time to meet the Lord of the universe face to face.

We'll continue to hold firm to the things you held dear-
To faith, unity, commitment and our vision so clear.

Fly on, my brother, fly on.
Fly home my brother fly home.
My brother, fly on home.

A Black Man's Ire

The black man in America is angry and justifiably so, for what man of any race was as long enslaved, as unmercifully worked and as little appreciated as he. What other man was rendered into bondage with such complete lack of regards, afforded not even recognition as a member of the species Homo sapiens.

What other man was wrenched as an infant from his mother's bosom, separated from his brothers and sisters, and as an adult, studded like any beast and forced to witness the wrenching of his own seed from the arms of the young mother, whom he himself was so unceremoniously thrust.

To exhibit the slightest hint of what is considered noble in a man, would subject him to myriad punishments of which beatings, castrations, lynchings, and burnings at the stake were only a few whatever the master felt most effective in discouraging other slaves so nobly inclined.

What demons of angst, fury, and unadulterated rage must needs be unleashed in the mind of the man forced to witness the molestation of his mother, his sister, even his daughter and oft times his mate.

And what man, pray tell, when formal slavery was abolished, would refuse to concede to the dictates of terrorism, jim crowism, racism and oppression_ moreover, would garner his forces to fuel the fire of the furnace, providing the creative energy to flourish despite odds insurmountable. Somehow he prayed and was heard by the Creator, who extracted a gem of love from the quarry of his animosity; and so healed his festering sores of hatred and indignation.

Brothers, draw nigh unto God and reclaim this blessing today. Let there be a recrudescence of the spirit of "the movement" for once again our anger is tempted as the ugly head of the oppressor is raised. America, as she struggles to maintain her self appointed position as moral mediator of the world, ironically seems obsessed with a penchant towards the politics of the good old days of white supremacy, as the self righteous mentality of the religious extremists turns deft ear to the word of God and locks arm to arm with the worshipers of hate.

O' but the wheels of justice keep right on 'aturning' in perfect harmony with the rhythm of God, oblivious to the chaotic clamoring of man.

So entertain not your anger, my brother. Moreover, unite, submit to the will of the Father, and resist evil wherever it is found. Draw nigh to God and he will direct your paths.

Dad's Departure

My father died exactly seven years prior to the 911 world trade center disaster. Strange, also is that at the exact time of his demise, family and friends were honoring my mother with a banquet celebrating her eightieth birthday. My parents had been separated for about ten years, and my father was in the hospital the victim of four years of Alzheimer's disease and superimposed intestinal problems. On the occasion of the banquet, well attended and joyous, I was asked to make some impromptu remarks. Usually fairly adept at this sort of thing, surprisingly I was overcome with tears as I reflected on the sacrifices and labors of my mother on behalf of her family. Perhaps these feelings of grief were for my father also,who at perhaps that very instant, was making his transition from life to death. As the news of dad's departure reached my younger brother James, a dentist in Connecticut, he called to make sure I had been informed. Lying in bed I told my wife Annie of dad's passing. Reflecting on his suffering for the previous four years ; I prayed that my heavenly father had accepted my earthly father into his kingdom. I thanked God also for blessing me with a dad who imparted so much inspiration to all of his children. As best I can recall,from what he told me, my father was born below Montgomery, Alabama, in or around Legrande, alabama,near the small town of Snowden, to Fannie Hampton and Charlie Franklin. Neither of his parents reared him, his mother moving on to Montgomery and his father, the local blacksmith deferred his care to an obscure, elderly black lady figure whom dad called simply "momma". Without former blood ties my father identified "momma" as his step-grandmother. She apparently was a powerhouse, a strict disciplinarian who raised my father in the face of abject poverty. They had love for one another. As a child my dad worked in the fields to help make ends meet as times were hard. Attending school sparingly he eventually dropped out in the tenth grade. About this time he had a close encounter with the law as he was caught running moonshine. He was pardoned as a first offender and shortly thereafter enlisted in the army at the age of seventeen. He told stories of discrimination in the army both at home and in Germany-how the women in the latter country requested to see the tales white soldiers had told them black men possessed. Though not formally educated my father was very intelligent and stayed abreast of current events. He obtained his high school diploma in night school upon returning home. My dad fathered five children with my mother, myself the oldest followed by my brother and three younger sisters. He was unique in that to my knowledge he was the only father in the housing project where I was reared, consistently spending time with his children. My brother James and I would await his arrival on Friday evenings, with lunch and all equipment necessary for our weekend joists packed, whether fishing or hunting the sport. After he showered and dressed we'd drive the twenty five miles or so to Legrande, Al., and adjoining landscape. In the two days we'd spend on the weekends, my father would constantly stress getting as much education as possible, and encouraged us to trust in our abilities. He insured we had no inferiority complexes. I thank my heavenly father for the earthly father he gave me. All accomplishments of myself and my siblings I attribute to the sacrifices and parenting geniuses of my mother and father. May God bless their souls.

"Hymn?"

Before you douche someone else's fire, make sure you have one of your own burning, lest you both freeze when the winter comes.
"hymn?"

Why does God allow his children to experience adversity?

1. To stop us in our tracks and get us off the express train to hell.
2. To serve as living testimonies as others see us overcome supernatural barriers, all to the glory of the Lord.
3. To prepare us to administer to others similarly afflicted.
4. To strengthen and harden us that we might bear what lies ahead.
5. To reveal and refine our hidden talents.
6. To develop within us trust in the Lord and not ourselves.
7. To teach us how to be thankful at all times.
8. To strengthen our faith as we learn to let go and let God.
9. For countless reasons God only knows.

Of Those Who Would Be Great

True greatness is inspired of God. It is the final destination and designation of all who hunger and thirst after righteousness and work unceasingly towards the Father's kingdom. Love for God dictates that we love our fellowman and demonstrate that love through service for others. The Master will bless all so lovingly disposed with the spiritual discernment, perseverance and power to succeed in all to which they aspire. Ultimately, they shall rise to greatness.

Let us set our sights first on the things of God and all others will be added unto us. When we enlist in the army of the Lord He will provide all the necessary skills and strategy, weapons and reinforcements for victory in battle.

Make us forever mindful, O'Lord, that just so long as we abide in your presence, nothing will prevail against us for stronger is he within than he without; and we can do all things through Christ who strengthens us.

may we develop, Father, the faith of david that we too might go on, wax strong, and grow great. O'Bless Your Holy Name.

Synopsis

A word spoken, a line read, can make the difference between
life and death, or success and failure.

A retired black general surgeon, raised by his parents in a
low income housing project of Montgomery, Alabama
with eight other siblings reflects on lessons learned and
nuggets extracted from a life infused with its fair share
of struggle, joy, pain, and ultimate victory.

Read, believe, and receive, and set sail on your own journey
to recovery.

About the Author

David C. Franklin, M.D., was born and reared in Montgomery, Alabama, where he attended Booker T. Washington high school and later received a Bachelor of Arts degree from Alabama State University. Dr. Franklin received the M.D. degree from the University of Alabama in Birmingham, 1974. He completed five years of General Surgical Residency Training, two initial years at Georgetown University, in Washington, D.C., and three subsequent years at York Hospital, York, Pennsylvania. Upon completion of his residency, Dr. Franklin returned to Birmingham and practiced general surgery for seventeen years, relocating to Plymouth, N.C. in 1996, where he continued his practice for nine years, finally moving to Elizabethtown, N.C. for three years before returning home to Montgomery, A.L. in 2007. Dr. Franklin is married to his best friend, Annie, and is the proud father of three children. He has twelve years experience working in men's ministry, both in Alabama and North Carolina. Semi- retired now, he busies himself with writing, speaking engagements and medical consultations. As a black general surgeon, Dr. Franklin was instrumental in integrating some six different hospitals. The numerous trials and tribulations experienced in the stead, he now counts as blessings for they were invaluable in his spiritual and charactual development. Dr. Franklin considers his greatest achievement the acceptance of Jesus Christ as his Lord and Saviour.

Printed in the United States
By Bookmasters